Student Well-being Series
Depression@College

BY DR DOMINIQUE THOMPSON

THE AUTHOR

Dr Dominique Thompson is a GP, young people's mental health expert, TEDx speaker, author and educator, with over 20 years of clinical experience caring for students, most recently as Director of Service at the College of Bristol Students' Health Service. It was for this work that she was named Bristol Healthcare Professional of the Year 2017.

She is a Clinical Advisor for the Royal College of GPs, and for Student Minds, the UK's student mental health charity. She was the GP member of the NICE Eating Disorders' guidelines development group, and the Universities UK StepChange and Minding Our Future committees. Dominique is also a member of the UK Mental Well-being in Higher Education group (MWBHE).

Dominique's TEDx talk, What I learnt from 78,000 GP consultations with college students, highlights some of the causes behind the recent rise in young people's mental health distress, and suggests ways in which everyone can better support the younger generation.

You can follow her on Twitter @DrdomThompson and on Instagram as drdom99

Rebecca Roberts is a licensed mental health counselor at a university in the US. Rebecca has over a decade of experience working in the college counseling setting. Additionally, she teaches new student programming, wellness, psychology and sociology courses at local universities. Rebecca has authored the book "Surviving _____ _____ ___ _____ _____ voted a lot of her work _____ ____ _____ _____ ___ __g students in their adju_____ _____ _____ ___ __ y and student life profes_____ _____ _____ ___ _____ ns of support.

First published in Great Britain 2019 by Trigger

The Foundation Centre
Navigation House, 48 Millgate, Newark
Nottinghamshire NG24 4TS UK

www.triggerpublishing.com

British Library Cataloguing in Publication Data

A CIP catalogue record for this book is available upon
request from the British Library

ISBN: 978-1-78956-091-6

This book is also available in the following e-Book formats:

MOBI: 978-1-78956-094-7
EPUB: 978-1-78956-092-3
PDF: 978-1-78956-093-0

Cover design and typeset by Fusion Graphic Design Ltd

Printed and bound in Great Britain by Clays Ltd, Elcograf S.p.A

Paper from responsible sources

TRIGGER™
The mental health & wellbeing publisher

www.triggerpublishing.com

Thank you for purchasing this book.
You are making an incredible difference.

Proceeds from all Trigger books go directly to
The Shaw Mind Foundation, a global charity that focuses
entirely on mental health. To find out more about
The Shaw Mind Foundation, visit
www.shawmindfoundation.org

MISSION STATEMENT

Our goal is to make help and support available for every
single person in society, from all walks of life. We will
never stop offering hope. These are our promises.
Trigger and The Shaw Mind Foundation

the *Shaw* mind
FOUNDATION

Creating hope for children,
adults and families

For Gareth. You're an inspiration – never give up.

CONTENTS

Introduction 1

Chapter 1: What is Depression? 4

Chapter 2: How Do I Know if I Have Depression and I'm Not Just Having a "Bad Few Days"? 13

Chapter 3: Tell Me More About Depression 19

Chapter 4: Types of Depression 22

Chapter 5: Are More People Getting Depression? 33

Chapter 6: Suicidal Thoughts and Feelings and Self-Harm 36

Chapter 7: I Think I Have Depression. What Do I Do Next? 43

Chapter 8: Helpful and Unhelpful Things People Do to Try to Alleviate Their Depression 52

Chapter 9: Behavior Boosters 61

Chapter 10: Talking Therapies 69

Chapter 11: Pills, Pills, Pills 73

Chapter 12: In Summary 79

Chapter 13: Where Can I Find Out More? 83

References 85

INTRODUCTION

Depression can be exhausting and disabling, and it can take over your life. You no longer feel like "you" and getting help can feel overwhelming.

Having to support someone with depression is common and can be stressful and demanding, so this book will be helpful if you are worried about someone else.

You've taken the first step by picking up this book! Well done. Keep going ...

Who Should Read This Book?

If you feel any of the following symptoms, you might be struggling with depression. Remember, you may have several of these symptoms at once. They may not be related to depression either, so talk to a professional if you:

- Feel numb, sad, down (depressed) or flat most of the time
- Regularly cry for no reason, or at things you don't feel you should cry about
- Feel inexplicably angry or irritable most of the time
- Think you are worthless or a failure
- Feel hopeless or helpless
- Feel tired all the time, even though you haven't done very much to tire yourself
- Wake very early every day or feel unrefreshed from sleep in the mornings

- Have started having "brain fog"
- Can't concentrate on your work or study or your focus is really poor
- Find it hard to make daily decisions, such as what to eat, what to wear, what to watch or do, and so on
- Have stopped caring for yourself or your appearance
- Have stopped doing things you used to enjoy
- Can't be bothered to do things if they're too much effort or your motivation is poor
- No longer enjoy life or the activities that you used to enjoy
- Have isolated yourself from people you used to spend time with because you don't want to be a "burden" to them
- Find that your appetite has gone or that you eat too much ("comforting eating")
- Have lost interest in sex
- Harm yourself to relieve your emotional pain or distract yourself from it
- Think about dying or believe that there's no point in being alive
- Think about ending your life, or believe that others would be "better off" without you
- Feel guilty for being alive or that you don't deserve to be happy
- Feel trapped or you can't see how life might get better
- Don't necessarily want to die, but don't want to be alive either

Why Should You Read This Book?

Reading this book will help you to:

- Learn more about what depression is and about the different types of depression
- Tackle some of the myths around depression

- Know more about self-harm and suicidal thoughts
- Learn about some of the causes of these feelings
- Consider whether you might have depression
- Know when and where to get help and who to speak to about it
- Better understand what help might be offered, and what might help you
- Understand which therapies are recommended for different types of depression
- Know what to try for yourself that might help, and what might make it worse
- Get a sense of which medications are available and what you might be offered, if appropriate
- Know where to get further help and check next steps

This book will tell you what you need to know if you have depression and / or if you self-harm or have suicidal thoughts because you are depressed.

> **Important point:** If you are struggling with your well-being, it is vital to let your university counselling center know what is happening with you. That way, they can make sure that you receive the right support and ensure fairness in any assessment they make of you and your work.
>
> Every college will have a process for what are called "mitigating" or "extenuating" circumstances (special circumstances that may have an impact on your academic performance, including physical and mental health issues, bereavement, and other significant life events). These can happen to anyone, so make sure that you let the college know. Talk to the disability services office on your campus, complete the necessary forms, and get the support you need and deserve.

CHAPTER 1

WHAT IS DEPRESSION?

Depression is not just "feeling sad". It is an illness that can affect your mood, thoughts, and behaviors.

In a Student's Own Words

A student who was a patient of mine wrote this in 2013 about how he felt when he was depressed. It explains, eloquently and movingly, how depression affected him (Studenthealth. blogs.bristol.ac.uk, 2013). Gareth is now recovered and works as a college lecturer; he speaks out about mental health issues in young people.

> I'm sick of waking up every morning and just being unbelievably tired. I never get to not feel tired, especially now. And it's so frustrating because when I'm not tired, or when I'm working well, then I'm actually pretty good. But when I'm not I'm just awful; I can't work and it's horrible. I literally have, very briefly, seen how good I can be, and that's always in my head somewhere being chased around and held down by being suicidal, and being always tired, and full of self-hatred and guilt and regret. I don't know how to get it out, or bring it to the forefront or anything. I think suicide is different now, it's not actively wanting to die, it's wanting to not exist, because existence is 90 per cent tiredness and guilt and regret and hate, and trying and failing to cover all of that up.   Gareth

This is such an emotional and descriptive expression of Gareth's depression, the exhaustion of just living through each day, and his negative thoughts about himself. It is important to say that depression does not always make you feel suicidal, but it can certainly lead to thoughts of suicide for some people. We will talk about that more later.

I hope that reading Gareth's description will help you to understand that you are not alone if you feel similar to this, or perhaps it might help you to better support a friend who you think is depressed.

'I found that with depression, one of the most important things you could realize is that you're not alone.'
Dwayne Johnson (*Serico*, 2015)

What Does Depression Feel Like?

You Feel Sad or Empty

For many people, depression makes them feel empty, numb, nothing, or just very sad, but not always about anything in particular. You might feel that there is no point in doing anything, like getting up out of bed or leaving your room or the house. You might feel there is no point in eating, washing, or dressing. You may believe that no one else cares about how you are feeling, or that you are not worth caring about. You might feel like a burden, that you are "in the way" of other people having a good time or living their lives, and that you're just an obstacle for them to have to deal with or manage. In short, you feel negative (or nothing) about almost everything.

You Are Angry or Irritable

Depression can also make you feel angry and / or *really* irritable and annoyed, with both strangers and the people you love. You might get angry at other shoppers in the supermarket, passengers on the bus, noisy kids in your street, or your family and friends or flatmates. Nothing they do is right – it all just gets on your nerves and can make you feel desperate or behave in an aggressive way. They may notice or comment that you are "snappy" or "moody", when in fact you are depressed.

You Are Indecisive

Depression can make you unable to make simple decisions. You might stand for ages in the local shop trying to decide which sandwich to buy, unable to choose and not really caring. You might not be able to decide what to watch on TV, or you could find that your attention span is affected; maybe you just flip from channel to channel or between different websites on your laptop. If you are asked what you want to eat you don't care; if your friends ask if you want to go out to the pub you just can't decide what to do.

You Are Tearful

Depression can make you tearful and you might find yourself crying most days – at your desk, in the library, playing sports, or sitting with friends. Sometimes it can be because of something sad on the news or a cute video, but often your tears and sorrow are for no reason. It's nothing you can explain, but sometimes a feeling of deep sadness may overwhelm you.

Your Sleep is Disrupted

Depression can affect your sleep patterns. You may want to sleep all the time, curled up under a the covers, hiding from the world, exhausted from doing nothing and feeling down. You may feel shattered and desperate for rest but unable to sleep. Your mind might be whirling or you might feel agitated. Sometimes depression makes you restless and unable to drop off to sleep. Sometimes it wakes you early (often at about 4.00am – it's even got a name: Early Morning Wakening. It's a well-recognized symptom), even though you are bone tired. Sleeping in the day feels like the only way to cope, but this can make sleeping at night even more difficult, and a vicious cycle is set up. You might find yourself sleeping too much – maybe for hours and hours, maybe half the day as well as the night, and yet still feel tired (or unrefreshed) when you wake up. It's exhausting.

You Might Use Cigarettes, Alcohol, and / or Drugs

Some people try to manage their sleep issues, irritability, and restlessness by smoking, drinking, and using a variety of non-prescribed drugs to cope. But while these may feel like a short-term fix, they will usually make a challenging situation much worse in the longer term. We will come back to this later.

Your Eating Patterns Are Disrupted

Depression can affect your appetite. You may find yourself wanting to eat a lot of fast food or "comfort" foods such as biscuits, toast, chocolate, cakes, and crisps so that you don't have to make much effort. The eating itself can be an act of self-care; you might try feeding yourself when you are ill, giving yourself treats to lift your mood. Sometimes you will feel better for a short while after eating such foods, but with time such a diet will make you feel stodgy, lethargic, and unhealthy, which could possibly make the depression worse.

Depression can, of course, make you lose your appetite. Loss of interest in activities can also include eating, and so sometimes making decisions about food can feel too difficult. You might avoid eating completely or just survive on foods like toast or chips – things that involve little effort but give a quick energy boost. Weight loss can follow swiftly.

Appetite changes are one of the reasons that those with depression often notice weight changes (both up and down) when they are low.

You Are Tired All the Time and Have Lost Your Motivation

Feeling "tired all the time" is so common among patients that doctors even have an acronym for it: TATT. It's a very real problem for people who are depressed. It can feel as if all the energy has drained out of you. Lethargy overwhelms you and you lose motivation or enthusiasm for many of the things that you have previously enjoyed doing, such as meeting up with friends, sports, reading, sewing, or being outdoors. Everything is too much effort. You stop going to club meetings, and hide in your room, or slump in front of the TV at best. Turning up for your Saturday job almost kills you, and going out with friends in the evenings is a no-go. Sex is of no interest. You make excuses to avoid going out, telling people you're "exhausted" and having a quiet one, but in fact you just can't drag yourself out. If it gets really bad, then even washing and looking after basic hygiene can become a problem for some depressed students.

You Feel Like You Have "Brain Fog"

For many students, one of the reasons that they finally seek professional support and help is because of the effect depression has on their academic work. They can no longer concentrate, focus, or study. They can't understand the texts they are reading and may have to read the same phrase or paragraph several times for it to go in. They find their memory is poor (made worse by their disrupted sleep) and they struggle to keep up with academic deadlines. Having been hard workers or high achievers and never really having "failed" at anything in the past, this particular aspect of depression can be a terrible blow for them. It may lead some to feel particularly down, think that they are failures, or even in some cases to think about suicide. The *depression* prevents them from seeing the world clearly and understanding that this is not "them" – this is the illness. It is affecting their brain and cognitive (thinking) processes.

You Feel Worthless, Guilty, and Ashamed

Being depressed can make dealing with other people a particular stress. Coping with other people's moods, expectations, and demands can be tiring at the best of times, so when you are feeling down it can be extremely challenging. Staying polite and patient, and even just replying in a civil manner can take it out of you. Some people might place expectations on you, such as to work hard or live up to past academic achievements. They may be supporting you in both financial and emotional ways, and you might feel that you can't – or don't want to – let them down. This is really tough. You have an illness called depression, but for lots of reasons it can be hard to admit this to people. You might not have realized yourself that you are suffering from it yet, so it can be tough to explain why you aren't feeling up to chatting or why you are struggling to keep up with your work and what you believe are their expectations. This can then make you feel more down and sometimes even worthless, guilty, or ashamed.

You Feel Agitated and Restless

As we have said, many people who are depressed feel slowed down or lethargic, but there are some who actually become more restless. They might pace, twitch, pick at their skin, and / or feel agitated. This is usually more likely in those who have the "angry" kind of depression, rather than the "sad" kind. It is also seen in bipolar depression, which we will describe later on.

You may notice yourself becoming increasingly irritated, aggressive, or uncooperative. In some cases you may become hostile or violent, though this is not always the case. It can feel like a build-up of pressure which you may try to get rid of by moving around or pacing. It feels very uncomfortable and should not be ignored.

You Have Poor Self-Esteem and Low Self-Confidence

As you start to feel down and the depression sets in, it may be that you turn some of that negative feeling on yourself. You may start to doubt or criticize yourself more. You might be harsh on yourself for not achieving the things you think you should be achieving, and this then can make you feel more down and possibly a "failure". You can get stuck on thoughts about yourself such as *I'm so hopeless and I can't even do this*, comparing yourself negatively to others around you. These first negative thoughts can lead to others such as *no wonder people don't want to be my friend if I'm this useless* or *I don't deserve to be happy / have friends / succeed*.

The vicious spiral of negative thoughts can be very hard to escape, and of course it continues to undermine your confidence in yourself and your ability to do things that you are perfectly able to do – and that you may have done well before, in fact. Depression can make you feel terrible about yourself, and even, in some cases, can cause you to hate yourself. Worst of all, it stops you living the life you should be leading, causing you to hide away from the world, avoiding people and activities you used to enjoy, and falsely making you believe that you are not a worthwhile and lovely person.

 You can have depression without feeling depressed; you might feel angry, or numb, but not sad or low. (RCPsych)

You Are Self-Harming

Sometimes when you feel very bleak the emotional pain can be so overwhelming that it leads you to physically harm yourself. The new physical pain may then distract you from the internal emotional pain for a while and give you something different to think about. This is how some people who self-harm describe the reasoning behind them harming themselves. Others describe their feelings as a "boiling pot with a lid on which is threatening to blow", and the self-harm is the equivalent of taking the lid off the boiling pot, releasing the pressure inside and allowing them to feel almost calm again.

The act of cutting, burning, and other ways of self-harming can give you a great sense of relief, but it is important to recognize that it is still a symptom of underlying distress. It can also be a high-risk activity as accidental fatalities can happen. Scarring, bleeding, and infection are all potentially serious consequences. Trying to deal with the emotional pain that leads to self-harm can be a positive step in the right direction for long-term well-being and health, although it can be very difficult to deal with.

You Have Suicidal Thoughts and Feelings

These are common. About 1 in 5 people will think about suicide at some point in their lives (Lee et al., 2010), but this will be covered in much more detail in a different part of the book to ensure that these thoughts and feelings get the time and recognition that they deserve. They can be scary or comforting, but the key thing here is to recognize them as a *symptom* of depression and not to ignore them, but to talk to someone about how you are feeling.

> 'It's difficult to describe depression to someone who's never been there, because it's not sadness. I know sadness. Sadness is to cry and to feel. But it's that cold absence of feeling – that really hollowed out feeling.'
> **J K Rowling** (*Oprah.com*, 2010)

Physical Symptoms of Depression

We have talked a lot so far about the emotions or feelings you can get with depression, and these are generally well recognized, even if it can take time to accept that you may need help. But it is less well known that you can suffer from physical symptoms with depression too.

The brain processes that cause us to feel sad, tearful, or angry can also upset other body pathways, such as pain and immune system pathways.

Pain Can Get Worse

It is therefore quite common for you to feel pain differently if you have depression, and those with chronic pain conditions can suffer particularly badly. Back and neck pain, headaches, and migraines can all get worse, as can digestive or tummy upsets and dizzy spells. We have already talked about sleep and appetite, and when these are derailed by depression, then physical health and energy levels will naturally go downhill too.

Immune System is Weaker or "Misfires"

There has also been a lot of research over the last few decades looking at how depression and the immune system interact, and it seems that while depression may weaken your immune system and make you more likely to pick up infections and illnesses (Hewlett, 2001), it is also possible that depression itself is an immune response, with stress (from life events, for example) causing immune changes in your brain, which can lead to depression (Nie et al., 2018).

All of these emotions, feelings, behaviors, and physiological changes can be symptoms of depression, so let's think together about when and how you might be able to ask for help.

> 1 in 6 people will suffer from depression at some point in their lives. (Verywell Mind, 2018)

CHAPTER 2

HOW DO I KNOW IF I HAVE DEPRESSION AND I'M NOT JUST HAVING "A BAD FEW DAYS"?

One thing that college doctors learn through experience is that everyone is different in how they describe depression, but there are also some things that many people have in common. Most students go to see the doctor when they can't think straight anymore, when their concentration, focus, and motivation are almost gone, and when they feel consistently flat, empty, or numb.

If reading through the lists and descriptions in this book makes you feel as though you are ticking off a checklist and saying 'Yes, yes, yes' to many of the symptoms, then you should take the next step, and talk to a trusted family member or friend – and then a professional – about how you are feeling. Help is available.

Ask Yourself This

It is important to recognize that we all feel some of these things sometimes, so the question to ask yourself about these feelings is this:

Am I feeling these things most or all of the time, most days, and for more than about two weeks? (In other words, are these difficult feelings pervasive and persistent?)

So, for example, if you have been feeling down, irritable, unable to sleep properly, and exhausted on most days for more than two weeks, then you should seek help and advice from a professional and support from a friend or family member. You may well have depression.

Similarly, if you have been crying most days for more than two weeks, or thinking that your friends and loved ones would be "better off" if you weren't around, then you should also seek support and advice without delay. This may also be depression, rather than just a "rough patch". Discussion with a professional will make clear what is happening for you.

'Depression is the most common mental health condition in the world, with 300 million people experiencing it at least once during their life.'
(World Health Organization, 2018)

Hiding the Symptoms of Depression

Some people may feel very low, sad, or irritable, but can manage to hide their feelings from those around them. They "put on a brave face" or mask how they are feeling, and they act in an apparently "normal" way day-to-day, but inside they are struggling and may feel quite desperate.

If you recognize yourself in this – if you are someone who tries to keep going despite feeling dreadful – then you are not alone. But it is still a really good idea to go and talk to someone about it. It is very common for students to be reluctant to show how they are feeling, as they may be worried about being asked to leave the college or stopped from studying their chosen course. But, in fact, if you seek help then the college should support you and offer services such as advice, therapy, or medical care.

'Going out and putting that happy smile on my face and singing the songs, honestly, sometimes it was like putting on one of those costumes, going out there and, underneath the costume, people don't really see what's going on.'
Liam Payne (Wootton, 2017)

Vocational Students

Particular groups of students on vocational courses such as medicine, dentistry, or veterinary sciences may be even more worried about declaring a mental health issue. They might try to push through their depression and suicidal thoughts because of their worries around "Fitness to Practice" and other similar policies.

It is really important to remember that in order to be a good, effective health care professional you need to look after *yourself* first, and that all the professional organizations, such as the General Medical Council and so on, are very clear that they actively support and encourage their colleagues to get help and show insight into their own needs for emotional support (gmc-uk.org 2015).

In other words, if you are depressed as a student, the college should support you, and if you are depressed as a vocational course student, your professional standards organization should respect and support you in getting help too – and so it will be seen as a positive thing for you to do.

Depression and Other Conditions

It is really common for people with depression to also have other problems to manage. Some of these may be mental health issues such as anxiety, and some may be long-term physical conditions such as diabetes. Let's think about what this might mean for you if you think this might be your situation.

Depression with Anxiety

If you are diagnosed with depression, you have a 1 in 2 chance of being diagnosed with anxiety too (World Health Organization, 2018). In other words, about half of students who have depression have anxiety as well. So, if you aren't just feeling down or flat but you're also worried all the time, on edge and nervous, then you may well have anxiety alongside your depression.

They will both need treatment, but the good news is that there are effective ways to manage both conditions together. This is also the case for depression with other *anxiety-related* disorders such as social anxiety, phobias, and obsessive-compulsive disorder. Don't ignore one of these conditions to focus on the other, or be misled into thinking you can't have both, because unfortunately you can. And it's common.

> Nearly **half** of those diagnosed with depression also have an anxiety disorder (adaa.org)

Depression with Other Mental Health Conditions

Students with eating disorders, schizophrenia, substance misuse conditions, and Attention Deficit Hyperactivity Disorder (ADHD) are also more likely to suffer from depression. It may be that having these conditions makes life harder in various ways and that is what leads people to feel depressed, or it may be that the depression is unrelated to the other mental health disorder and related instead to life events or genetic tendency.

If you believe you are one of these students, you will certainly need treatment and advice about managing your conditions in order to achieve your potential and navigate your academic and career pathways.

 Eating disorders and depression frequently occur **together**, as does depression and many other mental health problems, such as obsessive-compulsive disorder (adaa.org)

Depression with Physical Health Conditions

Doctors think it is important to bear in mind that any student coming to visit us with depressive symptoms might have an underlying *physical* condition, such as a thyroid hormone imbalance, diabetes, or Chronic Fatigue Syndrome. This fact does sometimes get overlooked in the day-to-day pressure of doctors' appointments, unfortunately.

Essentially, the thyroid gland sits in the front of the neck and produces hormones that are crucial for a healthy metabolism, including processes for weight management, energy levels, bowel function, and hair and skin changes, to name a few. So, when the thyroid gland stops working properly, it can *mimic* symptoms of depression and affect your mood directly. Thyroid disorders and depression often get mistaken for each other, but a simple blood test will clarify the cause of the symptoms.

Depression is also more common in other conditions such as diabetes and heart disease (Mental Health America, 2018) and is sometimes caused by particular medications, for example some tablets for acne, or certain brands of the contraceptive pill.

This is why it is important that if you are seeing a doctor for your mood, then you should also be prepared to answer sensitive questions about your physical symptoms, any medicines that you may be taking, and your family history of mental health issues.

 Up to 1 in 3 people with a long-term health condition such as diabetes or arthritis will also have depression (Naylor, 2012)

CHAPTER 3

TELL ME MORE ABOUT DEPRESSION

Causes of Depression

For those of you who would like to know a bit more about what might be *causing* your depression, this book will outline some of the current theories that are currently being investigated by scientists around the world. Other theories exist which describe behavioral causes, or the combination of biological, psychological, and social factors, known as the biopsychosocial theory of depression.

Does Depression Run in Families?

There does seem to be a lot of evidence that points to depression being inherited by one family member from another (Weitzman, Rosenthal and Liu, 2011), but it is unlikely to be a simple process. It is probable that you might have inherited a genetic tendency, and then certain factors in your environment as you grow up and develop affect whether or not you develop depression – and if so, how bad it may be.

 Women from BAME (Black, Asian, and Minority Ethnic) populations are more likely to suffer from depression than their non BAME female peers (Mental Health Foundation, 2018)

So, if your mom or dad had depression, it is more likely that you will also develop it, but this will partly depend on other influences from your surroundings and lifestyle.

Neuroplasticity Theory of Depression

This theory puts forward the idea that the brain develops according to influences from external stresses (Liu et al., 2017). Negative influences might include bereavement, loss, and emotional trauma in childhood.

It can help to imagine your brain like a bonsai tree. Normally the tree grows and the pruning that occurs to shape it would represent the normal "pruning" of nerve pathways. The theory states that negative stresses can then influence the pruning, causing the brain (tree) to grow in unusual or abnormal ways, creating new nerve pathways (branches), in particular allowing the area responsible for anxiety and fear (called the *amygdala*) to steadily grow larger.

Thus, your future reactions are disproportionately more negative as you grow older if you have a lot of negative influences on your brain development.

Some evidence shows that therapy and medication can re-set the nerve growth, but that will obviously take time, hence the need to keep going with any treatments that you start.

Immune Theory of Depression

This is the theory of how the immune system might affect your mood.

The guilty party in this theory is essentially a group of brain chemicals called "neurotransmitters", which *reduce* the making of serotonin and dopamine, two of the "happy hormones" in the brain (Raison, Capuron and Miller, 2006).

Cytokines also *increase* how much cortisol (steroid) hormone your brain produces and, as this is your "stress response" hormone used for regulating your blood pressure, blood sugars, and metabolism, your body will respond as if it is under stress. This affects sleep, appetite, weight, and your "fight or flight" reactions (Rakesh D., 2018). This may be partly why so many people with long-term conditions, like diabetes and arthritis, also suffer from depression.

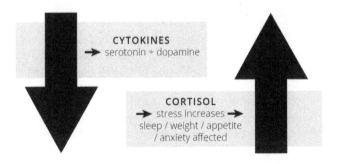

CHAPTER 4

TYPES OF DEPRESSION

Depression (Mild, Moderate, and Severe)

Depression is not about feeling "a bit sad or low" for a few days. It is a real illness and causes people to feel down, flat, empty, or numb, day in, day out, for weeks, months, or even years at a time.

It is important to say, however, that many people *continue to function* and go through the motions of life, work, and responsibilities, even when they are suffering from depression (usually mild to moderate), but they are likely to feel uninterested and unmotivated, lack enthusiasm, and, frankly, be irritable as they do so.

Not everyone with depression reaches the point of retreating to their bed or sofa and being unable to do the things they want to do – though when that does happen, it can be devastating.

Depression is generally described as being mild, moderate, or severe according to the range of symptoms, their persistence and pervasiveness, and how badly you are affected by them.

Treatment approaches for the three categories tend to be different, with mild depression generally needing mainly talking therapy for successful improvement, and moderate to severe symptoms usually requiring both medication and talking therapies. If symptoms are very severe, the sufferer may need medication to get them to a point where they can actually do talking therapy, because if you are severely depressed you may not be able to engage usefully in conversation and critical thought about your mood and what helpful steps to take next.

There are good screening questionnaires for depression, so when you go and talk to a counselor, psychologist, or doctor about your symptoms, it is likely that they will ask you to complete a brief series of questions about your mood, sleep, appetite, and thoughts of self-harm or suicide. This will help them to diagnose and classify your depression, and share with you a plan for treatment.

Real life example
Mild Depression

Sofia was halfway through her final year of studies and feeling under pressure. She was feeling pretty anxious too. She had noticed herself becoming irritable with her boyfriend and roommates and then feeling guilty. She had stopped going out quite as much, wasn't really as interested in sex anymore, and she was crying out of the blue at sad news or TV shows. On other days, however, she was able to get on with her work, join in her normal activities such as playing tennis, and sit around chatting with her friends. She couldn't quite work out what was wrong – was she being a grumpy person, or was there more to it?

She went to speak with a counselor and they talked about it. She completed a questionnaire and they chatted through the results. It seemed Sofia had mild depression, not bad enough to need a doctor's appointment or medication at this stage, but definitely at a level where counseling or a talking therapy such as CBT (cognitive behavioral therapy) might be helpful. A few weeks later – after having been for weekly sessions at the university counseling center, increasing her exercise, improving her sleep patterns, and reducing her alcohol intake – Sofia was feeling back to normal, on top of her academic work, and able to do all the activities she wanted to in the weeks before her final exams. She was glad she hadn't left it any longer before getting help, as otherwise she might have been more seriously unwell, and treatment would have taken longer, during a critical point in her studies.

Real life example
Moderate Depression

Bo was an international student and had been at the college for several months. He came to the doctor because he had lost a bit of weight and was not sleeping well. He was concerned he might have a physical illness, giving him what he described as a "brain fog", causing him to feel tired most of the time, and resulting in him feeling less hungry. He couldn't think as clearly and his work was suffering.

He was under a lot of pressure from home to do well at school, but was struggling to settle in with some aspects of his surroundings such as the weather, food, and language. He told the doctor that most days he felt "not himself" and there wasn't much let up in his negative feelings. He was either tired or irritable, and some weeks he just felt flat. He could still go to lectures, meet up with friends and so on, but he was not enjoying things anymore. He had briefly thought that life might not be worth living, but was not suicidal, although the thoughts had frightened him.

The doctor took time to explore the physical symptoms, as depression can lead to weight loss but other conditions such as thyroid disorders can get overlooked. They also discussed blood tests. They talked about possible emotional or psychological causes for his distress and planned to meet again when Bo had had time to think about such causes and his options for helping himself to get better though exercise, better sleep habits, good dietary choices, and minimal alcohol, as well as possible medication and therapy.

Over the next weeks and months they met regularly. Bo started seeing a psychologist for CBT and he slowly recovered from his depressive episode. His studies continued and he took more care to look after himself, as he realized how important this was to avoid a future similar situation.

Real life example

Severe Depression

Anika came into the doctor's consulting room slowly. She looked dishevelled, exhausted, and thin and did not meet the doctor's eye. Sitting on the chair, she stared at the floor and spoke slowly, answering the doctor's questions in a flat voice. She said she had come as a "last resort". She was feeling "numb" and wondered if there was anything the doctor could do to help. She had lost interest in everything. She had stopped getting out of bed most days, and was not showering. She couldn't remember when she last ate, but it was probably a day or two ago. She had thought about suicide a lot, and had cuts to her abdomen and thighs where she had harmed herself to relieve her emotional pain. Anika looked at the doctor with sad eyes and a hopeless expression.

They started to talk and make a plan. It was Anika's choice, but medication such as antidepressants would likely to be of benefit in a case of severe depression such as this. Then they would meet every week initially to check on progress and review the medication.

As Anika improved, she could start a therapy such as CBT. There were other support options available, such as online resources and peer-to-peer groups, and her friends were keen to help. Over the next few months Anika slowly improved, her mood lifted and returned to normal, and she was supported by her academic department to catch up with her work. Anika made a good recovery over time, and was able to fully engage with her studies and friends with the right kind of help.

'Let us shout it from the rooftops until everyone gets the message; depression has and nothing to do with having a bad day or being sad, it's a killer if not taken seriously.'
Ruby Wax (*Huffington Post*, 2014)

Seasonal Affective Disorder (SAD)

This is a mood change which can come over you as the seasons change (nhs.uk, 2018). As the days become darker for longer, the weather gets colder, and the winter sets in, it is not uncommon to notice a flatness of mood, an urge to stay in and "hibernate", a need to sleep a lot more, and eat more carbs. Weight gain can follow and feelings of guilt and hopelessness may come over you. Then, as the springtime arrives, the sun returns and the days get longer. Your mood lifts and suddenly all feels well again with the world.

It can take years for people to recognize this pattern of depression in winter. It may be worth thinking back over the times you have felt low in your life, and see if you spot a *seasonal* pattern.

 Depression is the leading cause of disability worldwide (WHO)

Real life example

Matt was a second-year postgraduate student, struggling with his workload. He came to see a counselor at his university's counseling center unsure of what help he needed. 'I think I'm turning into a hamster,' he said, still managing to smile weakly. 'I have so much work to do, but all I want to do is sleep, stay under the covers and eat junk food. And I have no interest in doing anything anymore.' The counselor listened and asked if Matt had felt like this before. It turned out that he had.

Every time the clock went back in the autumn and the days got shorter, all Matt wanted to do was hide away. He felt low and unmotivated, and it was proving disastrous for his academic work. They talked for a while; the advisor mentioned the possibility of SAD and some of the things that Matt might like to read about and try, such as more exercise, getting natural daylight each day, a lightbox (SAD light) on his desk in the mornings, perhaps CBT or even medication from a doctor if things were too difficult or not improving.

Matt was intrigued to realize that his symptoms had a name and that the seasonal pattern was key. He left the meeting feeling relieved and keen to try some of the suggested measures.

Bipolar Disorder

This book is mainly focused on depression, but it would be wrong not to mention a closely related condition called bipolar disorder (formerly known as manic depression).

People with this condition tend to have extremes of mood. A pattern develops, moving from depression and despair through to feelings of being very "high", "up" or overactive and extremely happy. Some sufferers may only rarely feel "normal".

Some people with bipolar disorder may experience psychosis; they might hear voices or see things that aren't actually there but which feel very real. They can be convinced of quite unusual beliefs when they are "manic", such as that they are a god or that they have great talents, for example exceptional musical ability or the ability to fly. At a less extreme level, before people become "manic" they may be considered "hypomanic".

In a manic phase, those with bipolar disorder may stop sleeping for days on end, feel very creative, see the world in brighter colors, and feel extremely energized. They can be reckless in many ways, even, unfortunately, allowing themselves to be vulnerable to danger. They may have a heightened sex drive and seek out sex with strangers, spend money they don't have, or phone friends in the middle of the night with "amazing" ideas, but actually make little sense to others. They might talk at great speed as their ideas race around their minds.

Am I Bipolar?

It is common for students ask the question 'Am I bipolar?' Many young people worry that they have bipolar disorder because they experience mood swings. It is therefore helpful and important to differentiate between normal mood ups and downs, which can occur *within* a day or a few days, and the persistent lows and then highs of bipolar disorder, which can each last for days or weeks at a minimum.

Bipolar disorder, when untreated, can make it impossible to function normally, to work and study, or have relationships. Sleep can be extremely difficult and you may stop eating. These more serious symptoms are unlikely to be present if you are having normal mood swings or even mild depression.

Those with mild depression can often worry it is actually bipolar if they have noticed that their mood is low, but then they have a good day or two when they feel productive and happy. As the depression at this stage is mild, it is not persistent every day, so it can be perceived as being interrupted by "up" phases which are actually just a normal mood. It is understandable that these young people then wonder if they have bipolar disorder, but talking this through with a doctor or psychologist will clarify the symptoms and patterns of mood, and should reassure the vast majority that this is not likely to be bipolar.

Most people with a manic phase (or early mania, such as hypomania) actually don't realize they are unwell until other people notice and advise that they need help. If in doubt, the following advice from Bipolar UK may be helpful (and there are also formal screening questionnaires which professionals may use to assess you): keep a mood diary / mood scale for a few weeks to monitor fluctuations and clarify whether there are extremes of high or low / suicidal mood. Take this with you to an appointment with a professional.

Real life example

Julia was a dental student, a high achiever with lots of friends and a very busy life at college. Her friends brought her to the counseling center one day as they were worried about her behavior. They explained that she was staying up for several nights at a time, writing what she said was music, but which made no sense to anyone else. They were also worried because she had been bringing various young men back to their room and having a lot of sex, which was out of character for her. She seemed to be behaving very excitedly all the time.

Julia agreed that these things were happening, but brushed them off because she felt "great" and was keen to share her thoughts about how her musical ability might lead the world to "be a better place". Over the course of the conversation it became clear that Julia had been depressed in the past, but that she had been feeling "up" for almost two weeks. She was not at all concerned about this.

It was agreed that she needed a medical assessment, and in time she was reviewed by a psychiatrist. She was diagnosed with bipolar disorder and a treatment plan was agreed. Her friends continued to support her, and her mom came to stay for a while as Julia started medication and talk therapy. She had a break from her studies and the college was very supportive of her as she recovered from her manic phase. In time she returned to her studies and was able to qualify as a dentist, while managing her bipolar disorder successfully and with support.

Grief, Loss, and Bereavement

It is normal when suffering from grief, loss, or bereavement to feel very (sometimes extremely) sad, to lose your appetite (and maybe a bit of weight), and be unable to sleep properly. We are only human, and humans have always mourned certain life events, such as the loss of a loved one, separation from our nearest and dearest, leaving home, or moving abroad. It may, as a process, actually help us to move on and heal from things too. Depression and grief can exist together, but it is important to allow a few weeks or even months after a difficult event has occurred before assuming that you should be feeling normal and well and functioning as you were before.

Sometimes students seek medical advice *the day after* a long-term relationship has ended because "I'm still crying, and I haven't got time to be sad". They have been unrealistic about how long a person needs to recover from loss and deal with grief. Clearly, in such situations we need to be kind to ourselves, allow ourselves to grieve properly for the loss of the relationship and our future dreams, and process such traumatic situations. We need to move on gradually.

One of the main ways to *differentiate grief from depression* is to look at whether the sadness, tears, and exhaustion gradually fade and are balanced by happy memories and an ability to rationalize the events with time, or whether the anger, guilt, and negativity is turned in on yourself, making you feel hopeless, worthless, and possibly even suicidal as time goes on.

Real life example

Jake was a first-year student who had arrived at college after a gap year. He told the therapist the story of that year, how he and his girlfriend had gone travelling after leaving school, and how, in a terrible bus crash, she had been killed a few weeks before he came to college. He was also injured, but after several weeks of treatment he had recovered well enough to come away as planned.

With the focus of the last few weeks on his recovery and then packing for college, he now wanted to talk about his grief at the loss of his best friend and partner.

He wanted to give time to dealing with his emotions at a challenging time of transition. He and the therapist were able to meet regularly as he settled into college life, dealing with his guilt at having survived the crash. He wanted to remember his girlfriend and make her proud of him while looking to his future emotional needs.

Jake did not become depressed, but he did have times of sadness, loneliness, and introspection when he would think about what might have been. He was also, with help, able to look forwards and manage his difficult emotions, allowing himself to thrive at college as the years went on.

 More women than men are affected by depression (World Health Organization)

CHAPTER 5

ARE MORE PEOPLE GETTING DEPRESSION?

There does seem to be a steady increase in the number of young people developing depression, according to studies in both the UK and the USA. Around 1 in 4 young women in the UK is now thought to be managing a "common mental health" condition, and depression is one of those conditions (NHS Digital, 2017). For young men the figure is stable at 1 in 10.

Why is That?

It seems fair to say that young people are under pressure like no previous generation. A whole variety of factors are combining to create what can feel like a "pressure cooker society", and it is no surprise therefore that more young people seem to be developing mental health conditions, with depression being one of the most common.

Competitiveness

We have become a society where even the fun stuff has become a competition. Baking cakes, photography, painting, singing and dancing; we now think of these as a type of "competitive sport". Whether it's done by kids at school or celebrities on TV, we are surrounded, worldwide, by relentless competition.

And this is particularly true in the college or college lecture hall and tutorial room, with the pressure on students no longer simply "to get a broad education" or even just a degree, but to get a First or top-class qualification, then a postgrad degree or other diploma, in a never-ending race to the top. This risks exhausting a whole generation.

Perfectionism

Closely linked to the overly competitive nature of our society is the documented rise in perfectionism among young adults (Curran and Hill, 2017). Perfectionism is striving for impossibly high standards and refusing to accept anything less than perfection. You can be highly self-critical and any mistake is unacceptable. The level of universal competitiveness seems to have driven a huge increase in the number of students with perfectionist traits in the USA, Canada, and the UK over the last 30 or so years. With perfectionist traits being closely linked to several mental health conditions such as anxiety, depression, self-harm, eating disorders, and obsessive-compulsive disorders, it starts to become apparent why I may be seeing more students like you with these conditions, through no fault of their own.

In trying to keep up with everyone else, trying to be *the* best – not just doing *your* best – might in some cases make you ill.

Social Media

So now let's magnify all of that competition and perfectionism with social media.

The lens of Instagram or Snapchat can really pile on the pressure. Not only are students driving themselves harder than ever before, but they are being "monitored" and "graded" 24 / 7 via their own social media channels. Social media in itself may not be causing depression in many cases, but it may be making a difficult situation worse. For some of you, social media *will* be the source of depression (e.g. seeing traumatic events online), or it might fuel obsessive tendencies and the seeking of reassurance, driving the need for "likes" or followers, or by playing into body image insecurities, making you feel worse. It's important to remember, though, that for a lot of people social media can also be a source of support and useful resources, particularly if they suffer from mental health problems that leave them feeling isolated and disconnected – it can offer a way of connecting with other people.

Other Stresses – for Example, Money

There are other significant stresses for you, of course, with academic pressure the number one cause of student distress and suicide, sadly (Research.bmh.manchester.ac.uk, 2018). These are closely followed by money worries, family issues, health problems, and relationship difficulties. Other stresses might include bullying, housing issues, and workplace issues.

Family and friends, who should be a source of support, can often be a cause of distress, for example through arguments with roommates, parental conflict or divorce, parental alcohol use, or friends' own mental health issues.

Loneliness and Isolation

These are relatively new issues for lots of students in a way they perhaps haven't been in the past. Many students are taking to the internet to write blogs about their lonely life, and so if you often feel isolated, then you are definitely not the only student feeling like this. Obviously if you are feeling depressed, that may make it harder for you to meet people, and then if you become isolated it can make your mood worse. So this can be a bit of a vicious cycle, but as you will see, there are ways to tackle this.

All these different pressures can really build up at a time of transition and academic expectation. It is therefore unsurprising that some students feel depressed and even suicidal much or all of the time.

CHAPTER 6

SUICIDAL THOUGHTS AND FEELINGS AND SELF-HARM

Self-Harm

Imagine a bubbling pot on a high heat on the stove in front of you. It's under pressure because it has a lid on it. Then imagine you take that lid off the pot. That sense of relief that comes from letting out the pressure and steam is how many people who self-harm describe the relief they feel from causing themselves physical pain and injury. They experience so much emotional pressure that hurting themselves physically allows some of that pressure to be released and a sense of calm to return, a sense of having things back under more control.

Other people who self-harm say that the physical pain *distracts* them from the emotional pain temporarily, giving them a brief sense of peace and creating a diversion from their psychological distress.

Self-harm is many things to many people, but it is essentially a way to cope with internal emotional pain when that emotional pain is too great to endure. It can take any form, but common methods include cutting the skin, burning, scratching, and pinching, as well as taking overdoses of medications or non-medical chemicals such as bleach. Some people punch hard surfaces to hurt themselves, and others pull out their hair.

It may be a regular coping strategy, something that some students do every time things feel overwhelming, or it may be a rare and occasional activity, to distract and survive the unbearable challenges that life throws at us. Some people self-harm just to feel "something, anything" because they feel so numb inside. Self-harming is *not* a "phase", "attention seeking", a "teenage thing", or "being melodramatic" (Knightsmith, P 2018).

Why Does Self-Harm Matter?

It can be very hard for those who don't self-harm to understand why someone might take such action, but it is important for us all to try to remember just how bad someone will be feeling emotionally for them to want to physically harm themselves as a distraction.

Self-harm is actually an important "symptom" too of course, a sign that someone is suffering, possibly silently, and that they may be depressed or anxious, have an eating disorder, have a personality disorder, or be coping with other distressing issues.

Therefore, if you are someone who self-harms, it would be common for you to *also* be suffering from other mental health problems, so it is strongly recommended that you seek help from a kind and compassionate professional in order to explore what you are feeling, what may have led to the self-harm and any other difficulties you may be managing by yourself or with support from family and friends.

Self-harm may seem like it brings relief, so it may feel like it's a logical reaction if you are feeling dreadful. But unfortunately it is also a *high-risk* activity, meaning that people who self-harm are also more at risk of suicide (Klonsky, May and Glen, 2013) or accidental death, so it is strongly recommended that you address the issues that are leading you to seek physical pain.

What Help is Available?

There is lots of help available to help people who self-harm, both to support them with the underlying issues that have led to it and to help them when they feel like self-harming, or to distract them when they feel desperate. Some brilliant apps and websites exist and are listed in our Resources section, alongside phone and text support lines. And then, of course, there is actual psychological therapy (between three and twelve sessions are recommended by NICE, the National Institute for Health and Care Excellence) which you can try, to help you move forwards and deal with your problems.

Speak to your doctor for a referral to a psychologist or specialist team for this psychological treatment.

Try this

When you are feeling like you might harm yourself, try to distract yourself by thinking of your favorite song lyrics and repeating them in your head.

An alternative is to call someone who loves you and who will be supportive even if they don't know how you're feeling right now. Have a chat with them – the urge to self-harm will pass and you can relax a little.

Suicidal Thinking and Behavior

When life feels unbearable, pointless, futile, or worthless, it is not uncommon to consider whether you really want to keep going, to stay alive, or to bother with life. You might say things like 'What's the point?', think you are a burden to others, and you may feel "trapped" in your life, aimless, and unmotivated to carry on. All of these thoughts can lead you to consider taking your own life, and such suicidal thoughts can be very frightening and exhausting.

It may be helpful to know that up to 1 in 5 people will have suicidal thoughts at some point in their adult lives (De Leo et al., 2005), but for most people these are fleeting thoughts and are often just in response to overwhelming stress. They settle and pass and we move on with our lives.

For most people who think about suicide, the negative feelings (feeling worthless, useless, unwanted, or numb) will be temporary and the person will go on to lead a life with normal ups and downs, but they will recover from the suicidal thinking. It is important to remember that even such difficult thoughts can be tolerated and managed, then left behind, in time. The key is to talk to someone you trust.

Help for Suicidal Thinking

If the thoughts are more persistent, however, or plans start to form in your mind, or you prepare for taking your own life (such as by stockpiling medication, writing a note, reading about methods online, or giving away your pet) then it is *really important* to seek help and talk to a professional such as a counselor, doctor or psychologist on the *same day*, especially if these thoughts are escalating or feel overpowering.

I need help NOW!

Immediate help is always available if you feel like this. Dial the emergency phone number 911, speak to your doctor, or go to the local hospital emergency department. Organizations like National Suicide Prevention Lifeline are also available at 1 (800) 273-8255.

Specialists and therapists *want* to hear from you, that is what they are there for, and so please do let them know if you are feeling like this.

Safety Plans

Something that a lot of people are now doing and finding helpful is writing themselves a "safety plan" for use when times feel dark or thoughts become very negative again.

Safety plans are a tool (a set of instructions if you like) that you can turn to, and you might have created one when you weren't feeling too bad, preferably with the support of a professional or even a college personal tutor.

The idea is to make a list (on paper, on your phone / laptop, or on specially designed apps) of specific activities to try when you feel yourself going down into a spiral of negativity. It can include useful resources, phone numbers, and websites, as well as trusted people to contact and speak to if life feels overwhelmingly difficult at that moment. The plan should be kept somewhere you can easily find it if needed, and should start with noting the signs to look out for that you are going downhill emotionally. List some activities that always make you feel a bit better (going for a walk, listening to a particular song, or watching a funny show) and then list the people to contact, and emergency numbers if needed.

It can help to give yourself written instructions of how to keep yourself safe ("give roommate stockpiled medication") and also to include some positive reasons for living (your family, your pet, your love of music) and so on. You can share the plan with a trusted friend or family member if you like.

Finally, you should commit to trying to use the plan, though it is not a contract – it is just a commitment to yourself to read it and act on it when you are down.

Try this

Make your own Safety Plan now

	Safety Plan
What makes you think about harming yourself (triggers)?	
Reasons for living	
Making things safe e.g. removal of access to means	
Activities that improve your mood	

	Safety Plan
Activities to calm yourself	
Contacts (general support)	
Contacts (suicide and self harm prevention specific)	
Contacts (professional e.g. doctor / counseling service)	
Contacts (emergency)	
Personal commitment to implement safety plan	

CHAPTER 7

I THINK I HAVE DEPRESSION. WHAT DO I DO NEXT?

A lot of help is available at college and in the healthcare system, though sometimes finding the right person to help you can be tricky.

It is common to hear students (and sometimes their parents) comment that someone at the college "should have known" that they were depressed or unwell, but it is important to remember that universities usually have tens of thousands of students to support, so there is more of an expectation that, as young adults, college students will reach out for support if they need it.

So, if you are unsure, then it is absolutely fine (and welcomed, in fact) to reach out and ask for advice or help, even if you think you might be wasting people's time. Nobody minds! They would much rather see students at an *early* stage of distress or concern than wait for things to become worse and potentially disastrous.

> The big message here is *please talk to someone* –
> a friend, family member, academic advisor, spiritual advisor, counselor, psychologist, or a doctor.
> They are all there to support you and help.
> *Please. Talk to them!*

'You don't have to struggle in silence. You can be un-silent. You can live well with a mental health condition, as long as you open up to somebody about it, because it's really important you share your experience with people so that you can get the help that you need.'
Demi Lovato (Ryan, 2017)

Friends and Roommates Supporting Each Other

It is well recognized that the first person many students will talk to about mental health or well-being worries is a friend or roommate. This is fine in general, as long as the friend is okay with it and not overwhelmed by the scale of your issues or their own problems. So, if the person you talk to seems keen to support you but also asks you to seek professional help, please listen to them and book an appointment. They may be feeling worried about you or have stuff going on that you don't know about, or they may have personal expertise – for example, from an experience that you are unaware of (perhaps their mom had depression). They might then recognize the signs that require expert advice.

Either way, while it is fine to talk to friends first, they are not experts nor are they objective, and they also have their own lives to juggle. So do support each other, but please also talk to the professionals.

College professionals available for mental health support

- Counselors
- Disability Support Services
- Student Health Centers: Doctors and nurses

- Mental health nurses (Community Psychiatric Nurses)
- Psychologists
- Well-being advisors
- Psychological well-being practitioners
- Psychiatrists

> People identifying as LGBT+ are more likely to suffer from depression
> (Mental Health Foundation, 2018)

So why doesn't everyone with a mental health or psychological concern seek help? What is stopping many of the students who are suffering with anxiety, depression, or other symptoms, from approaching any of these people or resources? Because sadly a significant number of people with mental health issues *do not* seek help.

Reasons You Might Not Ask for Help
(Czyz et al., 2013)

- You don't think that you need help or you may not recognize that you have symptoms
- You haven't got time to seek help, and it might interrupt your studies
- You hope that you can sort it out yourself and don't feel you need professional help
- You fear stigma or discrimination from others
- You stigmatize yourself (i.e. you are harshly critical of yourself for having these issues) (Boerema et al., 2016)
- You don't think you have had the problems for very long, in your view
- You worry that other people won't be supportive and understanding
- You lack trust in professionals and you worry about confidentiality

- You worry that professionals that you talk to will lack expertise in the topic (Berridge et al., 2017)
- You don't believe in biological (medical), or psychological-based explanations for mental health issues (Van Voorhees et al., 2006)
- You have previously experienced poor quality support or treatment

Let's explore these reasons in a little more detail, as these may be what is standing between you and a healthy, depression-free life!

You Don't Think that You Need Help, or You May Not Recognize that You Have Symptoms

One of the most common questions that I'm asked by young people is 'How would I know if I have a mental health problem?'. Essentially the answer is that if you don't feel well, you think something is wrong, or you are not getting the things done that you would expect or need to do (such as your work or meeting people and making friends) – or if you are worrying that any of this is happening – then *talk to a professional* to check it out. You have nothing to lose, and that's what they are there for.

Well-being and healthcare professionals are trained to ask the right questions and put it all together. Then they'll share their opinion with you about whether or not the feelings you are having are in fact normal and to be expected, or whether you need additional support or even treatment.

If you don't feel right, then don't suffer in silence. Talk to someone. It is good to talk to friends and family of course, but that may not be quite enough if you are still anxious. So, try to talk to someone who has experience in working with mental health problems.

And talking to professionals is confidential.

You Haven't Got Time to Seek Help and it Might Interrupt Your Studies

Maybe we should switch this round and say, 'You haven't got time to be unwell.'

Life is busy, there's no doubt about that. But without your health and, in particular, your psychological health, then it's going to be tough to do all the amazing things you want to do, especially while in college. So go on – take five minutes to go online, register with whichever service you want to talk to, and make an appointment. It may be the best thing you do this year.

You Hope that You Can Sort it Out Yourself, and Don't Feel You Need Professional Help

Well, it is certainly not unreasonable to try to help yourself before seeking professional help, of course, but if you have given it a month or so – using reliable, credible, professionally written resources (see relevant section at end of this book) – then it is probably time to run it past a trained counselor, psychologist, or doctor.

There are loads of brilliant self-help options to try, from books to apps to online resources, and being able to say that you tried them first will also show how motivated and engaged you are, so that's a bonus. But everyone needs help sometimes. We are humans, and evolved to be social creatures, so give yourself a break and allow yourself to be supported by other (compassionate) humans.

You Fear Stigma or Discrimination from Others or You Stigmatize Yourself (i.e. You Are Harshly Critical of Yourself for Having These Issues)

Stigma and discrimination – if it's not other people, then we do it to ourselves. As if life wasn't tough enough, other people criticize us (or we fear that they will) for being human and having emotions, which sometimes get a little overwhelming. The only way to fight this one is to push past their (and sometimes our own) judgemental comments (real or imagined) and ask for help anyway. You are worth it.

Other people's opinions may be ill-informed and narrow minded, so you shouldn't value or listen to what they say anyway. You can do this!

You Haven't Had the Problems for Very Long, in Your View

If you've had the issues for more than a month, and especially if you've tried to help yourself along the way, then you really shouldn't wait any longer before talking to someone. Life is precious and you shouldn't spend it at the mercy of your mental health issues. There are fantastic and effective treatments out there, so don't spend any more time struggling. Also, you may have to wait on a waiting list for a bit, so best to get signed up and get in line, if that's the case.

You Worry that Other People Won't Be Supportive and Understanding

It can be difficult to predict how people might react when you tell them you are struggling or need help, but sometimes they will support you and be more understanding and supportive than you might expect. Even if they are less helpful, try not to let that stop you looking after yourself and getting the help you need.

Sometimes the people we care about most are unable to be as fully supportive as we might hope, but that is their issue, not ours. We can only take responsibility for our own lives.

You Lack Trust in Professionals – You May Be Concerned About Confidentiality

Health and well-being professionals all work to *strict standards of confidentiality*, and have their own professional guidance about keeping information confidential, which they follow carefully. No professional should share your information without discussing this option with you first, and in very limited circumstances they will consider sharing it if it is in your best interests.

In the rare cases when a professional needs to share your information without your agreement (consent), it would only be if you or someone else was considered to be in immediate (usually life-threatening) danger. They will do their best to seek your consent in these cases too. They cannot share information with future employers and you will *always* be asked for your consent before medical information is requested or shared, and that includes for the Armed Forces.

For example, if a person develops a psychotic condition (they lose the ability to recognize that they are ill) and they are likely to hurt themselves or someone else, then a healthcare professional may have to disclose information. And, as mentioned, they will try to obtain consent *before* doing so. The same would be true for suicidal thinking or if a person was considered to be at high risk of severe self-harm.

Students do worry about the sharing of their confidential information, but this is rarely done, and certainly not without consent. It is only done in circumstances where the student themselves will benefit and have given their consent, for example to plan better therapy or to ask for a second, expert opinion.

You Worry that Professionals that You Talk to Will Lack Specialist Expertise in the Topic

The people who choose to work with students, such as those in college support and health services, do so because they specifically enjoy working with young people and usually have additional training and expertise in the issues that most commonly affect young adults. For example, 50 per cent of consultations in college health centers are for a mental health problem (IPPR, 2017), and so the doctors working in these locations tend to have a great deal of experience in managing mental health issues.

They will often work closely with specialist doctors such as psychiatrists, and with psychologists. The college counselors and well-being practitioners are similarly highly trained, and stay up to date with both mandatory and voluntary training programmes and appraisal.

All of these professionals are familiar with the wide variety of mental health issues that affect young people, and have specialist skills to help them manage the students' individual problems. In fact, college counseling and health services are probably the most expert teams in caring for student mental health issues.

You Don't Believe in Biological Counselling-Based Explanations for Mental Health Issues

Some people have a different understanding of emotional difficulties, perhaps believing it to be a spiritual issue, for example. Clearly it is up to each individual to think about their well-being in terms that they are comfortable with, and it may be helpful to read about mental health on reliable and credible websites (see Resources section of this book), or in relevant books, if greater clarity and understanding are desired. But whatever your belief system for explaining mental health issues, there is help available to you.

Many universities have a chaplain, or religious or spiritual leader, for the campus community, who is often linked to local leaders of many faiths and backgrounds, so connecting with them might be a good first step in talking to someone empathic and compassionate about your depression. Chaplains, or other faith leaders, are happy to talk to students of all faiths, and those who follow none, and many students find it helpful to talk to someone caring and who understands campus life despite not being a healthcare or academic professional at the college. Whatever your beliefs, start the conversation and see if that helps to relieve some of your worries.

You Have Previously Experienced Poor Quality Support or Treatment

Everyone's experience of care is different, and can depend on a whole variety of factors such as waiting times, reception staff interaction, the attitudes and beliefs of the professional, or treatment side effects or results (benefits and failures). If you have had a previously poor experience, that is a real shame that it was negative. However, the good news is that trying something new or different, or even the same treatment with a different person, can have a different outcome.

Keep an open mind about the type of talking therapy offered, the nature of the therapist, the use of medication, or talking to friends and family about your experiences. Advances in medicine and therapy are made all the time; guidelines are updated and protocols developed.

What you were offered before may not be what you are offered again. Moving to a new clinical counselor or therapist may be a step change for you, and lead to different, even brilliant, results.

It's got to be worth considering, hasn't it?

CHAPTER 8

HELPFUL AND UNHELPFUL THINGS PEOPLE DO TO TRY TO ALLEVIATE THEIR DEPRESSION

There are, of course, many things that are well recognized to improve your mood, and it's important to try to give them a go if you can, as they may help you at a difficult time. Avoiding doing these things or engaging in behaviors such as drinking too much alcohol or taking drugs such as cannabis will undoubtedly make mood disorders worse, so it may be helpful to talk to a professional about your personal situation and what actions you can take to improve things.

Some of these suggestions may not have occurred to you before, or you may initially think *Uh-uh, no way!* But keep an open mind, and let's see how we get on ...

Exercise

We all know exercise is good for us, and that it boosts our "happy hormones" in some way, and in fact research has shown that exercise can be enough to help some people overcome depression. But if you feel depressed, it can be near impossible to motivate yourself to get out there and do stuff. So be kind to yourself. Go for a walk, maybe in a part of town or the countryside that you haven't visited before.

As a student, it's easy to stick to the same old routes and areas that you know, but I advise you to branch out, go into the residential areas, the parks, the waterfronts, and the great outdoors, and this will also neatly tick off another fantastic way to feel better which is ...

Try this

Look at the tourist website for your college town or city and pick a recommended area to visit and walk around, maybe even join a walking tour for an hour or two. Then explore that new area on foot – it will distract you and get you outside and exercising, which is all helpful when you're feeling low.

'To those struggling with anxiety, OCD, depression: I know it's mad annoying when people tell you to exercise, and it took me about 16 medicated years to listen. I'm glad I did. *It ain't about the ass, it's about the brain.*'
Lena Dunham (Dunham, 2015)

Go Outside

Being in nature is a really good way to feel better. Sometimes just experiencing "weather" (it doesn't have to be sunny) can blow you around a bit and make you feel something other than down or flat. It can take you away from your thoughts, distract you, and pass the time. There is something restorative and refreshing about walking or running outside, by water, up a hill, under trees, or just lying on the grass, staring at the sky. It connects you with the world around you and shifts perspective. At an absolute minimum, it ensures you get your vitamin D each day if you are outside for 20 minutes with some sun on your skin! Bonus!

'Wherever you are, at any moment, try and find something beautiful. A face, a line out of a poem, the clouds out of a window, some graffiti, a wind farm. Beauty cleans the mind.' **Matt Haig** (2016)

Eat Well (and Minimize the Alcohol!)

When you feel down, sometimes the easiest thing is just to stop eating or eat crisps and junk food. It's minimum effort, provides a few calories and the body is kept alive … and while this exhausted and depressed way to sustain yourself is totally understandable, it probably isn't helping your mood and it may actually be making things worse.

So, try to choose simple things to eat that still involve minimum effort while you're recovering, but are perhaps a little more helpful to your well-being.

Just as a reminder, alcohol is a depressant – in other words, it will actually make you feel more down and will make the quality of your sleep poorer, so the less you drink the better you will feel overall.

Alcohol is a depressant and will make depression worse, but is often used by people trying to numb their feelings of despair. This creates a vicious cycle. They feel worse, so they drink more. The same is true for drugs such as cannabis.
(Alcohol and Drug Foundation, 2018)

Get a Plant (or a Pet!)

Being a student means it can be really difficult to have something that you can nurture and care for in the privacy of your own room like a dog, but a lot of students have told me how having a plant to look after, or even a pet goldfish, hamster, or rat if allowed, has transformed their lives.

Humans are generally nurturing and enjoy looking after others, so caring for another being (whether animal or vegetable) can be uplifting and boost your happy hormones (like oxytocin). It's important to check the rules of wherever you are living, of course, and ensure that you have the time and energy to care for the plant or pet. But if you can, it might be the change that helps you turn the corner and lift your mood.

Try this

Buy a pot plant for your room, something robust and resilient (not an orchid, unless you have particularly "green fingers"!) to care for day-to-day. Read up about what attention and watering it needs and really make an effort to look after it properly. You will feel a bit more connected to the world, and it will brighten up your room, bringing the outside in!

Real life example "Pet Therapy"

Bethany was a second-year student and finding her course challenging. She was in a hectic, noisy, shared house with flatmates and had a pretty strict (non-pet-friendly) landlord. At home she had had lots of pets and was used to the company of animals, but at college she really missed her non-human support network. She chatted with a welfare professional at the college as she noticed her mood getting lower and her sleep becoming erratic. She told them about how she missed her pets, and so they suggested that she consider volunteering at an animal shelter, advertising to college faculty and staff, and doing just enough to bring her comfort but not enough to interfere with her studies. Bethany was thrilled with the outcome, as her regular dog walks were helping out the staff who cared for her at college and she benefited from the pets as therapy. Her mood lifted over the following weeks and she continued more energized through her second year.

Help Others

In the same way that nurturing a pet can help you feel better, helping others directly can also be beneficial. When you are very depressed it can feel almost impossible, but you might start just by "being in the room", for example literally being present at a charity event cake / book sale, supporting a friend doing a 5K run for a favorite charity and so on, and then you might feel like doing something yourself, for example working a couple of hours for a charity organization.

Longer term, activities where you help others, for example helping children to learn to read, or collecting funds for non-profit organizations, can really give purpose to your life and make you feel good about yourself. And you meet new people!

Face Time

No, not the screen version – real "human to human" face time. People have evolved to thrive when connecting with others, and we do best when we share experiences with other humans. It can be difficult, with rising loneliness and more of us spending time on our screens, to really meet people and connect with other humans, but if you can, call up or message a good trusted friend and then just sit and chat (no phones). You will feel better for it, and it costs nothing.

It can be a real challenge to reach out when you feel down, so maybe start with a message to let them know you are struggling and would appreciate their support. People love to help others (see point above) so when they realize you aren't feeling great, a good friend will want to support you.

Try this

Just sitting with someone else or going for a walk, side by side – not necessarily talking – can be therapeutic. If they are good at listening, and you feel able to talk, then that's a great combination. If you don't feel like talking yet, then just walk and experience being outside and getting some exercise.

'If you know someone who's depressed, please resolve never to ask them why. Depression isn't a straightforward response to a bad situation; depression just is, like the weather.

Try to understand the blackness, lethargy, hopelessness, and loneliness they're going through. Be there for them when they come through the other side. It's hard to be a friend to someone who's depressed, but it is one of the kindest, noblest, and best things you will ever do.' **Stephen Fry**

Sleep Rules!

Sleep must be one of *the* most underrated "activities" that humans can do to heal themselves! The importance of sleep as a process, and how we "miss it and mess with it" at our peril, needs to be emphasized.

There are some basic sleep rules to help us get the most out of this therapeutic pastime, so even if you do nothing else, trying to get your sleep back on track will be beneficial.

Try this

The Rules

- Try to go to bed and get up at the same time every day, Monday to Sunday.

- Try to be asleep when it's dark and awake when it's light, although within reason – for example between 11:00pm and 7:00am without sleeping in the daytime or staying up all night to work.

- Stop all work and turn off all screens one hour before bedtime.

- Spend that hour winding down, chatting with a friend, listening to quiet music, taking a shower, reading quietly, or watching TV (nothing too scary or exciting!).

- Exercise in the daytime before about 6:00pm, and don't have caffeine or alcohol late in the evening, nor eat any ready meals.

Stick to these rules for about 4–6 weeks, and if that isn't working, check out CBT-I (which is CBT for Insomnia, an evidence-based technique to improve sleep). Make time to talk to a professional about how you are doing, as there may be other things that can help improve your sleep and mood.

Real life example

Nic was a final-year student who came to the doctor as a last resort, as is often the case, unfortunately. He had become very low, numb, and irritable with his roommates over the last few months and his girlfriend had "ordered" him to seek help. He wasn't sleeping and it was exhausting both of them. He would stay up late working, often until 3.00am, and then would try to sleep but be unable to relax. He would drink alcohol or smoke weed to try to lull himself into a sleepy state, but although it would work sometimes and get him off to sleep, he would then only sleep lightly and wake irritable and annoyed a few hours later. Being too exhausted at that point to get up, he would then sleep into the daylight hours and the cycle would begin again the next night.

Nic and the doctor had a long chat about the issues affecting him; his mood, his drinking, weed smoking and so on, and they pulled together a picture of his current mental state. They agreed that the first things to do were reduce the alcohol intake, especially before bed, cut out the weed altogether, and then, over the next four weeks, adopt a strict sleep routine. The doctor explained all the "sleep rules" and gave him a pamphlet about them. They agreed that they would meet again in four weeks and review Nic's progress.

Nic went away, and, with the support of his delighted girlfriend, he set about improving his daily habits. As the days passed and his new sleep routine settled down, he found himself being asleep when it was dark and up when it was light. His head felt clearer, his memory improved, and his brain fog lifted. His mood was still low but he could now motivate himself to work in the daytime, and he started talking to a counselor. His full recovery took another few months, but tackling his sleep was the first step.

Avoid Drugs

It is totally understandable that when life is stressful, you might want to block it out or take something to help you feel different or possibly better. When you take stuff you have found yourself, such as alcohol or drugs, it's called "self-medicating".

It doesn't usually work out well unfortunately, so if you are at this stage, then it's definitely time to talk to a counselor, psychologist, or doctor about your worries.

Long-term use of cannabis has also been shown to reduce motivation, concentration, and the ability to organize your thoughts, which the Higher Education Center for Alcohol and Drug Misuse Prevention and Recovery "can cause particular problems for students".

CHAPTER 9

BEHAVIOR BOOSTERS

If you think you have depression or are generally feeling low, you'll more than likely notice that you've stopped doing the things you used to enjoy. Where you used to exercise regularly, attend study groups or meet up with friends, you now find excuses to stay in your room in front of Youtube or Netflix. Even the thought of catching the bus to college or chatting to other students, including your flatmates, makes you feel exhausted. Depression depletes energy and saps the enjoyment and sense of achievement you get from activities. In turn this starts a "vicious cycle" of not putting any effort into doing things or avoiding doing things, and therefore not getting anything back – no enjoyment or any sense of achievement!

To remedy this, you can use a **Behavior Booster** – scheduling some activities into your week that you have previously enjoyed and / or from which you used to get a sense of purpose or achievement. Getting outside, exercising, and talking to friends etc. will help you feel better, and these are all examples of Behavior Boosters. Behavior Boosters have been shown to be an effective strategy in boosting mood and helping overcome depression (Dimidjian et al., 2006), and if you are waiting for CBT to start, it is likely that they will have you do this as the first step in treatment anyway!

Let's look at this idea in more detail using an example.

Jon used to attend a study group at the library. He enjoyed it for the social interaction and chatting to other students on his course, but also it gave him a sense of doing something productive. Recently Jon started feeling pretty down and low, and he was finding it really hard to motivate himself to go to classes and attend the study group. He forced himself to go to the study group last week, despite preferring to stay in his room and sleep. He found he didn't enjoy it as much as he used to, and although in chatting to other students was okay, he didn't get as much of a buzz from it. Plus, he didn't feel like he learned as much as other weeks – perhaps because he was finding it hard to pay attention. This week he is still feeling pretty low in his mood, so he has decided to skip the study group and just stay in his room instead.

Using a series of contiuums we can see that before Jon was depressed, he enjoyed the study group a lot (8/10 with 10 being the maximum enjoyment), it didn't feel like much effort to go along (3/10 with 10 being maximum effort), and he felt like he had achieved something (7/10 with 10 being maximum achievement).

Before feeling depressed

Jon enjoyed study groups (8/10)

It took little effort to go to study group (3/10) – as in he was motivated to go and it didn't feel very hard to get there

And he got a sense of achievement after attending the study group (7/10)

Now let's look at the same scale when Jon began to feel down and when he last went to study group.

Jon got less enjoyment out of going to study group (3/10)

Jon found it much more effort to go to study group (8/10)

And he got a lower sense of achievement after going to study group (5/10)

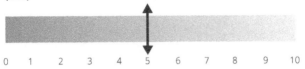

Now you'll see some of the scales are the opposite for Jon; he got little enjoyment from attending study group, felt as if he had achieved less as he normally did, and he had to make a much bigger effort to actually get to the library to attend the group.

So you can see this is why people stop doing the things they enjoy as it takes so much more effort to get such little enjoyment or they feel less effective; it hardly seems worth it the effort!

So if we examine the situation now, in the middle of depression, let's see what happens when Jon simply avoids going to the study group:

Jon gets no enjoyment out of study group

It takes Jon no effort to avoid things

Jon also gets no sense of achievement from doing nothing

Jon is not getting *any* enjoyment or sense of achievement from study group! That seems a pretty bad outcome when you think about it. If Jon was able to make a big effort and attend this week, he might be able to extract that little bit of enjoyment out of going – 3/10 is still better than 0/10 for enjoyment! He might also find that it wasn't as bad as he had predicted, and that he maybe even got more than 3/10 along the enjoyment scale. Similarly, He will still get a sense of achievement from going to study group, even if he found it hard to pay attention and didn't learn as much as he would usually when he is feeling better.

Using these scales is an excellent way of showing yourself that, while you might only experience a small amount of enjoyment or get less of a sense of achievement from an activity compared to what you used to when you were feeling better, it is better than having no enjoyment at all and feeling ineffectual. From this you can then devise a diary in which you can plan a few activities ahead – nothing too heavy or too taxing, but small things that help you reconnect with the pleasures you once enjoyed, or to feel effective again. It is also helpful also to think about what you might need to do in order to achieve these things – such as telling a friend so they can check in with you how you went, or even join you for the activity. Setting these small, achievable goals is an excellent way of lifting your mood and feeling better.

To help, fill in the box below. You should select activities that you used to enjoy, or ones that gave you a sense of being effective or achieving something:

Table 1: *Design your own Behavior Booster*

The activities I would like to do this week are ... (e.g. go for a 10-minute jog, attend my psychology lecture)

I plan to do these activities on the following days at the following time (e.g. Wednesday afternoon at 10:00)

After the activity describe how it went below. How much effort did it take? How much enjoyment did you get from it? Did you get a sense of achievement?

Mark your rating from 1 to 10

Enjoyment ⬭ Effort ⬭ Achievement ⬭

What things might help me to achieve these goals? (e.g. asking my friend to join me, setting my alarm)

If you are struggling with depression and feeling low, please try a Behavior Booster. It seems like a simple idea, but it really works! Look at the study group example we've shown you and see how attending even if you don't feel like going is still more rewarding than staying at home. Behavior boosters really do work, and this is what a psychologist or counselor is likely to ask you do in the first place anyway. So get ahead of the game and try it yourself first!

CHAPTER 10

TALKING THERAPIES

You Have Options

A variety of non-medication options are available (and evidence-based) for the treatment of depression. In other words, talking therapies work for depression in most cases.

This means that when you talk to a healthcare or counseling / psychologist professional about your symptoms and what your options are for getting better, you might discuss self-help (exercise, books, websites, and so on), mindfulness, and individual and group therapies. Within the latter options, you might be offered CBT (Cognitive Behavioral Therapy), psychodynamic psychotherapy, interpersonal or other specialist therapeutic approaches (SIGN Guidance, 2010).

What is Cognitive Behavioral Therapy (CBT)?

We've talked a bit about CBT. So, let's take a closer look at how it can help. The aim of CBT is to change the way we respond or behave in response to what we are thinking and feeling.

CBT is a really effective approach for depression issues. It looks at the links between the events in our lives, how we interpret those events, and our responses to them.

Cognitions are the ways we think, what we believe, and how we interpret things. The way we feel is our emotional response to these things. And our *behaviors* are what we do in response to them, mentally or physically.

For example, *I am a failure* as a thought (cognition) can lead you to feel sad, numb, and unable to do the things you want to do. This leads you to think you are even more of a "failure" (this reinforces the negative thoughts), and so it becomes a vicious cycle. This is sometimes called a "negative thought spiral".

CBT tries to break this cycle by training your mind to have a *new* reaction to negative thoughts and eventually to change the negative thoughts.

If we change your thoughts, you can change your reactions and your behaviors. It may also work on tackling challenging situations you find yourself in, or physical symptoms in response to stress.

It is *not* a quick fix, and you may have to work hard by keeping a note of feelings, thoughts, and actions between sessions. Your therapist will help you with this.

It focuses on the present, not the past.

Because everyone is different, and everyone's depression is different, there is no single solution, and it may take a couple of tries to find the right thing for you. CBT for depression can be delivered in many ways – self help books, group or individual CBT session with a trained therapist and these days there are online options and computerized CBT too, so don't be surprised if they are offered to you.

You may be able to self-refer to free psychological therapy services. Check with your college counseling center to see if they provide online programs in conjunction with therapy such as TAO, a therapy assistance online program that can be used as a self-guided tool consisting of education and interactive modules, practice tools, journals and progress measures.

The Therapist

The therapist as a person and their personality, approach, and field of expertise are also clearly important factors, so don't rush in and feel you have to commit to therapy with someone if you're not comfortable with them or confident with their knowledge.

Check they are working with an organization you trust or that they are registered with a nationally recognized professional membership organization. Speak to them or meet them at least once before committing to a series of sessions with them.

Waiting Lists

There can sometimes be a wait for therapy, so it may be that in the meantime you try online support with resources provided by your college – ask about free "bridging" support to get you through the waiting period. There may be drop-in sessions just to have someone to chat to when you need it.

Your doctor is always an option if you're feeling bad and in need of support, and of course all universities have a variety of pastoral support, so check their website ("student support") for mental health advisors, well-being advisors, pastoral tutors and accommodation / residential staff who can help you while you wait for treatment.

Remember

The thing to remember here is that for *mild through to severe* depression, talking therapies are recommended –

sometimes alongside medication – so it is really important to know that you *can* get better, even if it takes a bit of time to see the improvement with treatment. Don't give up – talking therapies can be hard work sometimes, but are really effective, and definitely worth trying.

CHAPTER 11

PILLS, PILLS, PILLS

These are some of the things that people say when discussing medication for depression, as reasons not to take them:

But here's something to think about ...

You rarely hear people say those things about Type 1 diabetes, or asthma, or cancer.

People are very much more worried about being judged for taking medication for mental health problems than they are for physical health problems, which can make it really challenging for those who are keen to try something and are open minded about options. They might then feel criticized for not "beating" an illness without medical assistance, despite the fact we would not expect people to "beat" Type 1 diabetes without insulin.

Depression is a complex mental health illness which has shown clear and repeated benefit from medication over many years of scientific trials, and sufferers should feel able to try medication if they are advised to do so by a qualified professional and if it feels appropriate in their individual situation.

'We would never tell someone with a broken leg that they should stop wallowing and get it together. We don't consider taking medication for an ear infection something to be ashamed of. We shouldn't treat mental health conditions any differently.'
Michelle Obama (Obama, 2016)

Antidepressants are recommended for moderate to severe depression, but not mild depression.

In fact, in a recent study of 21 different antidepressant medications and more than 116,000 people, it was conclusively proved that medication was *more effective* than placebo for moderate to severe depression (Cipriani et al., 2018).

In other words, the pills do work, but it's really important to find the *right* one for you – with the least possible side effects – if you are going to take them. Even if one type doesn't work, another might be great for you.

The advice here is to talk to a doctor, perhaps one with an interest in mental health or young people's health, and discuss your symptoms. You can also discuss whether medication might be an option for you. For many people it is unnecessary, but for others it can be transformational and literally life changing.

Some people need medication to sleep, function, balance their mood, and be well enough to try talking therapies. For others it lifts them out of suicidal thoughts and reduces the need to self-harm.

Try to remain open minded about anti-depressants and other medications for mental health conditions. As most of them will show whether or not they are working and are right for you within four weeks, and as side effects for most will also settle in that time (best to start with low or half doses for a week or so, to minimize side effects – ask your doctor), you can quite quickly see if you want to carry on with them or not, or change to a different brand and so on.

> **Try this**
> When you are waiting for treatment to start working (or to start at all) it may help to take one day at a time, doing small activities that nurture your soul. Try doing something like cozying up on the couch and watching your favorite funny movie or getting a receipt and trying to cook something you've never made to feel productive and treat yourself to something tasty. Drawing or coloring in can also feel peaceful when you are very low and have no energy for more organized or demanding activities. Just one day at a time, sometimes one hour at a time, is all you need to focus on.

Starting, Stopping and Safe Approaches

Certainly 6–8 weeks will be enough to give any medication a good "go", and if you don't like them, and if it's only been eight weeks or less, you can stop them gradually over 1–2 weeks. If you've been on them longer, the weaning period will be proportionately longer too (6–8 months of treatment, for example, will need 6–8 weeks weaning off to avoid withdrawal side effects). This is standard advice by the American Psychological Association.

Tell your doctor that you are stopping and the reasons for it if you decide to do so independently, so that they can note it for future record. Then if you do decide to try them again in future, they will know that a particular brand didn't suit you the last time and to try something different.

Common Myths and Misunderstandings About Antidepressants

They're addictive

Modern antidepressants are not addictive. People worry about this a lot, but if you take them, you will need them for a period of time, just like you would antibiotics for an infection, then you will stop after a recommended medication course length.

In general, first-time treatment courses are for six months minimum, and if you need them for a relapse in future the course length is usually two years minimum. Some people do need longer courses than this, but most don't. You don't get addicted to them in that time (in other words: increasing doses are not needed to have the same impact; they don't cause cravings and they don't act quickly), but you may need to stop them gradually to avoid withdrawal side effects.

Withdrawal (discontinuation) effects can include tummy upsets, electric shock sensations, anxiety, flu-like symptoms, and headaches. They are common, but can be minimized by reducing your dose very slowly over a reasonable period of time. So taper the dose and wean off gradually!

Don't stop antidepressants suddenly if you've been taking them for more than 6–8 weeks.

Side effects are dreadful

All medications can cause side effects. This is one thing that students ask about a lot, of course, but they sometimes forget that even headache tablets can have side effects for some people. So yes, side effects can be common, but are usually mild and settle quite quickly, especially if you start by taking *half* of the recommended treatment dose for at least a week. Discuss this with your doctor before starting.

Side effects include jitteriness, headaches, sleep disturbance, anxiety, nausea, diarrhea, and problems with having or enjoying sex (sexual dysfunction), so do ask about the particular medication you are being prescribed and what the issues might be.

Most of the side effects wear off after a week or two, but not all, so if they are intolerable it is important to go back and discuss this. Different types of antidepressants have differing side effects too, so a switch to an alternative type may be all that's needed.

And they don't "change" who you are as a person or your personality; they help you to get back to normal and feel like yourself again.

If the first one doesn't work, none will

Many students have to try more than one type of anti-depressant before finding the right one for them. But when they do, it can really transform their lives and they are so pleased that they persevered to find the one that suited them and works best.

I'm feeling better, I think I'll stop now

A common issue is that as the medication starts to work after a few weeks, people feel themselves return to normal and are keen to stop the medication. And so they do, believing themselves to be "cured" and the problem sorted. Unfortunately, the evidence is that antidepressants need to be taken for several (between 6 and 12) months after feeling better to have a sustained long-term benefit, so stopping them too early will likely lead to you relapsing and needing to take them again, or even feeling worse overall.

It's so important to embrace the improvements but not to stop taking the medication too soon. Just keep going, live your life, get on with your studies and activities, and keep checking in with your doctor, then plan to come off them when you have been feeling well and "normal" for at least six months (RCPsych.ac.uk).

People who have a second episode of depression in their life will need to take them for two years after feeling better, and if you have a third episode you may need to take them for a few years. But everyone is different, so it's best to chat through with your own doctor of course.

So actually, the drugs do work!

In summary, medication is not for everyone or for every type of depression, but they do work in many cases and should definitely be considered on an individual basis after you've discussed them carefully with a professional and considered the side effects and withdrawal planning for when you're ready to stop.

CHAPTER 12

IN SUMMARY

It may be helpful at this point, before we look at where you can find out more, to recap some of the key points about depression in case you are struggling or know someone who is.

Depression is truly awful, and when you're "in it" it can be hard to see out. But it does *not* have to be awful like this in the future. You *can* get better.

It takes time, and you may need to try different types of talking or tablet therapy before you get there, but depression is a treatable illness. You just need to find the treatment that works for you and stick with it.

So many students say they wish they had asked for help sooner when they realize that their symptoms and feelings can be sorted out, addressed, and treated with the right professional help. Don't delay! Please talk to a professional soon.

Facts

- 1 in 5 people will suffer from depression at some point in their lives
- More women than men are affected
- Nearly *half* of those diagnosed with depression *also* have an anxiety disorder

- Eating disorders and depression frequently occur *together*
- Up to 1 in 3 of people with a long-term health condition such as diabetes or arthritis will *also* have depression
- You can have depression without feeling depressed; you might feel angry, or numb, but not sad or low
- People identifying as LGBTQIA+ are more likely to suffer from depression (Mental Health Foundation, 2018)
- Women from BAME populations are more likely to suffer from depression than their non-BAME female peers (Mental Health Foundation, 2018)

Getting Help

- Try the resources in the next section to learn more about depression, or to hear from people who have experienced it and can share their thoughts on how best to manage it
- Talk to family or friends for everyday support
- There are lots of self-help options for depression: exercise, being in nature, nurturing a pet or plant, connecting with others and helping them too, as well as mindfulness techniques, so start with these to see if you can take steps for yourself. You'll feel good for trying, and there's always more help if you are struggling
- Try a Behavior Booster for as a first step. it is an easy way to help us feel better and is very effective
- Your college will provide some free help, for example in the counseling or well-being services
- Look at your college *Student Support* services website as a first step to see what they can offer, or your health center

- Many universities offer free online support too, so that's another option to consider if you aren't keen to talk face-to-face yet

Therapy Options

- Lots of help is available, through talking therapies or medicines
- The main thing is to take the first step and talk to a professional about your options
- No one will make you do anything you don't want to do
- Services are confidential, so you can speak freely and share your worries
- Therapy such as CBT (Cognitive Behavioral Therapy) will almost always be the first line treatment you are offered where available: this will involve a course of talking sessions
- You may be offered group sessions, which can be a good first step for depression, if the waiting list for one-to-one support is long
- If you try the talking therapy and it is not working even after a recommended amount of time, or your symptoms are severe and disabling, you may be offered tablets (medication) to help the talking therapy to work better
- Medication can work very well and effectively for depression and there are many different types to try, depending on your problems
- You may need to take medication for several months. It is important not to stop it suddenly if you have been on it for longer than 6–8 weeks
- A doctor should always be happy to discuss your personal situation and come to a decision with you about which medicine may be worth trying, as well as discussing potential side effects, how long to take them for, and any other concerns you may have

- If the first type of medication you try does not work well for you, don't give up; chat with your doctor and consider other options
- They should then review you regularly to check all is going well

CHAPTER 13

WHERE CAN I FIND OUT MORE?

General Resources

- **National Institute of Mental Health** (NIMH) provides information on statistics, clinical trials and research. NAMI references NIMH statistics for our website and publications. Phone: 1-866-615-6464

- **The Suicide Prevention Lifeline** connects callers to trained crisis counselors 24/7. They also provide a chat function on their website. Phone: 1-800-273-8255

- **The American Foundation for Suicide Prevention** provides referrals to support groups, mental health professionals, resources on loss and suicide prevention information. Phone: 1-888-333-2377

- **Anxiety and Depression Association of America** (ADAA) provides information on prevention, treatment and symptoms of anxiety, depression and related conditions. Phone: 240-485-1001

- **SAMHSA Treatment Locator** provides referrals to low cost/sliding scale mental health care, substance abuse and dual diagnosis treatment. Phone: 800-662-4357

Depression

Websites

- Active Minds **www.activeminds.org**
- Mental Health America **www.mentalhealthamerica.net**
- National Institute of Mental Health
  www.nimh.nih.gov
- American Foundation for Suicide Prevention
  afsp.org
- The Trevor Project – mental health support for LGBTQ+
  students **www.thetrevorproject.org**
- Depression and Bipolar Support Alliance (DBSA)
  www.dbsalliance.org

TEDx Talks

- "Why Big Boys Don't Cry" by Gareth Griffin
- "What I Learnt from 78,000 GP Consultations with
  College Students" by Dominique Thompson

YouTube

- Pooky Knightsmith on Mental Health videos

Books

- *Reasons to Stay Alive* by Matt Haig
- *Mad Girl* by Bryony Gordon
- *Sane New World* by Ruby Wax
- *The Stranger on the Bridge* by Jonny Benjamin
- *Overcoming Depression* by Paul Gilbert

Apps (all free)

- *Better Stop Suicide* – a suicide prevention self-help app
- *Headspace.com* – meditation guides for a wide range
  of problems
- *MindKit* – a widely recommended mental health app
- *My Coping Plan* – for writing your own safety plan

REFERENCES

Adaa.org. (n.d.). *Depression | Anxiety and Depression Association of America, ADAA*. [online] Available at: https://adaa.org/understanding-anxiety/depression [Accessed 25 Jan. 2019].

ADF - Alcohol & Drug Foundation. (2018). **ADF - Drug Facts - Cannabis, Weed, Marijuana**. [online] Available at: https://adf.org.au/drug-facts/cannabis/ [Accessed 17 Sep. 2018].

Bipolar UK. (2018). *I think I might have bipolar*. [online] Available at: www.bipolaruk.org/Pages/FAQs/Category/i-think-i-might-have-bipolar [Accessed 14 Oct. 2018].

Cipriani, A., Furukawa, T., Salanti, G., Chaimani, A., Atkinson, L., Ogawa, Y., Leucht, S., Ruhe, H., Turner, E., Higgins, J., Egger, M., Takeshima, N., Hayasaka, Y., Imai, H., Shinohara, K., Tajika, A., Ioannidis, J. and Geddes, J. (2018). Comparative efficacy and acceptability of 21 antidepressant drugs for the acute treatment of adults with major depressive disorder: a systematic review and network meta-analysis. *The Lancet*, [online] 391(10128), pp.1357–66. Available at: www.thelancet.com/journals/lancet/article/PIIS0140-6736(17)32802-7/fulltext [Accessed 25 Oct. 2018].

Curran, T. and Hill, A. (2017). Perfectionism is increasing over time: A meta-analysis of birth cohort differences from 1989 to 2016. *Psychological Bulletin*. [online] Available at: www.apa.org/pubs/journals/releases/bul-bul0000138.pdf [Accessed 28 Sep. 2018].

Dbsalliance.org. (2014). *Understanding Agitation*. [online] Available at: www.dbsalliance.org/pdfs/brochures/agitation.pdf [Accessed 24 Sep. 2018].

De Leo, D., Cerin, E., Spathonis, K. and Burgis, S. (2005). Lifetime risk of suicide ideation and attempts in an Australian community: Prevalence, suicidal process, and help-seeking behavior. *Journal of Affective Disorders*, [online] 86(2-3), pp.215–24. Available at: https://pdfs.semanticscholar.org/7607/f6d9276ff71f222d87378a7bd31bae902318.pdf [Accessed 25 Oct. 2018].

Dimidjian, S., Hollon, S. D., Dobson, K. S., Schmaling, K. B., Kohlenberg, R. J., Addis, M. E., and Atkins, D. C. (2006). Randomized trial of behavioral activation, cognitive therapy, and antidepressant medication in the acute treatment of adults with major depression. *Journal of Consulting and Clinical Psychology*, 74(4), 658.

Dunham, L. (2015). *Lena Dunham on Instagram: "Promised myself I would not let exercise be the first thing to go by the wayside when I got busy with Girls Season 5 and here is why: it…"*. [online] Instagram. Available at: www.instagram.com/p/1WoYh8C1GY/ [Accessed 23 Jan. 2019].

Gmc-uk.org. (2015). *Supporting medical students with mental health conditions*. [online] Available at: www.gmc-uk.org/education/standards-guidance-and-curricula/guidance/supporting-medical-students-with-mental-health-conditions [Accessed 28 Sep. 2018].

Haig, M. (2016). *REASONS TO STAY ALIVE*. Leicester: Thorpe.

Hewlett, K. (2001). *Can low self-esteem and self-blame on the job make you sick?*. [online] www.apa.org. Available at: www.apa.org/monitor/julaug01/jobsick.aspx [Accessed 24 Sep. 2018].

Klonsky, E., May, A. and Glenn, C. (2013). The relationship between nonsuicidal self-injury and attempted suicide:

Converging evidence from four samples. *Journal of Abnormal Psychology*, [online] 122(1), pp.231–37. Available at: www.ncbi.nlm.nih.gov/pubmed/23067259 [Accessed 25 Oct. 2018].

Knightsmith, P. (2018). *Dr Pooky Knightsmith*. [online] pookyh. Available at: www.inourhands.com/skills-building/what-not-to-say-if-your-child-is-self-harming/ [Accessed 25 Oct. 2018].

Kroenke, K., Spitzer, R. and Williams, J. (2001). The PHQ-9. *Journal of General Internal Medicine*, [online] 16(9), pp.606–13. Available at: www.ncbi.nlm.nih.gov/pubmed/11556941.

Kübler-Ross, E. and Byock, I. (1997). *On Death and Dying*. Simon and Schuster.

Lee, J., Lee, M., Liao, S., Chang, C., Sung, S., Chiang, H. and Tai, C. (2010). Prevalence of Suicidal Ideation and Associated Risk Factors in the General Population. *Journal of the Formosan Medical Association*, [online] 109(2), pp.138–47. Available at: www.ncbi.nlm.nih.gov/pubmed/20206838 [Accessed 24 Sep. 2018].

Liu, W., Ge, T., Leng, Y., Pan, Z., Fan, J., Yang, W. and Cui, R. (2017). The Role of Neural Plasticity in Depression: From Hippocampus to Prefrontal Cortex. *Neural Plasticity*, [online] 2017, pp.1-11. Available at: www.hindawi.com/journals/np/2017/6871089/ [Accessed 28 Sep. 2018].

Medlineplus.gov. (2012). *Tips for Getting A Good Night's Sleep | NIH MedlinePlus the Magazine*. [online] Available at: https://medlineplus.gov/magazine/issues/summer15/articles/summer15pg22.html [Accessed 12 Dec. 2018].

Mental Health America. (2018). *Co-Occurring Disorders And Depression*. [online] Available at: www.mentalhealthamerica.net/conditions/co-occurring-disorders-and-depression [Accessed 28 Sep. 2018].

Mental Health Foundation. (2018). *Mental health statistics: LGBT people*. [online] Available at: www.mentalhealth.org.uk/statistics/mental-health-statistics-lgbt-people [Accessed 17 Sep. 2018].

Mental Health Foundation. (2018). *Mental health statistics: black, Asian and minority ethnic groups*. [online] Available at: www.mentalhealth.org.uk/statistics/mental-health-statistics-black-asian-and-minority-ethnic-groups [Accessed 17 Sep. 2018].

Naylor, C. (2012). *Long term conditions and mental health*. [online] Kingsfund.org.uk. Available at: www.kingsfund.org.uk/sites/default/files/field/field_publication_file/long-term-conditions-mental-health-cost-comorbidities-naylor-feb12.pdf [Accessed 25 Jan. 2019].

Nie, X., Kitaoka, S., Tanaka, K., Segi-Nishida, E., Imoto, Y., Ogawa, A., Nakano, F., Tomohiro, A., Nakayama, K., Taniguchi, M., Mimori-Kiyosue, Y., Kakizuka, A., Narumiya, S. and Furuyashiki, T. (2018). The Innate Immune Receptors TLR2/4 Mediate Repeated Social Defeat Stress-Induced Social Avoidance through Prefrontal Microglial Activation. *Neuron*, [online] 99(3), pp.464–79.e7. Available at: www.cell.com/neuron/fulltext/S0896-6273(18)30531-2 [Accessed 24 Sep. 2018].

Obama, M. (2016). *First Lady Michelle Obama: Let's Change the Conversation Around Mental Health*. [online] HuffPost UK. Available at: www.huffingtonpost.co.uk/michelle-obama/lets-change-the-conversation-around-mental-health_b_9245816.html [Accessed 24 Jan. 2019].

Oprah.com. (2010). *The Brilliant Mind Behind Harry Potter*. [online] Available at: www.oprah.com/oprahshow/the-brilliant-mind-behind-harry-potter/all [Accessed 24 Jan. 2019].

Pathways.nice.org.uk. (2013). *Self-harm – NICE Pathways*. [online] Available at: https://pathways.nice.org.uk/pathways/

self-harm#path=view%3A/pathways/self-harm/longer-term-management-of-self-harm-assessment-and-treatment.xml&content=view-node%3Anodes-interventions-for-self-harm [Accessed 25 Oct. 2018].

Raison, C., Capuron, L. and Miller, A. (2006). Cytokines sing the blues: inflammation and the pathogenesis of depression. *Trends in Immunology*, [online] 27(1), pp.24–31. https://www.cell.com/trends/immunology/fulltext/S1471-4906(05)00288-7?_returnURL=https%3A%2F%2Flinkinghub.elsevier.

Rakesh, D. (2018). *The immune system and the pathogenesis of depression*. [online] Medium. Available at: https://medium.com/lazy-synapse/the-immune-system-and-the-pathogenesis-of-depression-8b0ab5725965 [Accessed 24 Sep. 2018].

Rcpsych.ac.uk. (2009). *Antidepressants: key facts from the RCPsych*. [online] Available at: www.rcpsych.ac.uk/pdf/antidepressants.pdf [Accessed 27 Oct. 2018].

Rcpsych.ac.uk. (2018). *Cannabis and mental health*. [online] Available at: www.rcpsych.ac.uk/mentalhealthinfo/problems/alcoholanddrugs/cannabisandmentalhealth.aspx [Accessed 14 Oct. 2018].

Rcpsych.ac.uk. (2018). *Depression: Key Facts*. [online] Available at: www.rcpsych.ac.uk/healthadvice/problemsanddisorders/depressionkeyfacts.aspx [Accessed 17 Sep. 2018].

Research.bmh.manchester.ac.uk. (2018). *Centre for Mental Health and Safety (College of Manchester)*. [online] Available at: http://research.bmh.manchester.ac.uk/cmhs [Accessed 28 Sep. 2018].

Ryan, L. (2017). *Demi Lovato on Boxing, Eating Well, and Speaking Up About Mental Health*. [online] The Cut. Available at: www.thecut.com/2017/02/demi-lovato-on-boxing-eating-well-and-mental-health.html [Accessed 24 Jan. 2019].

Serico, C. (2015). *'Have faith': See Dwayne Johnson's inspiring advice for people with depression*. [online] TODAY.com. Available at: www.today.com/health/dwayne-rock-johnson-shares-inspiring-message-people-depression-t56586 [Accessed 24 Jan. 2019].

Sign.ac.uk. (2010). Non Pharmaceutical Management of Depression in Adults. [online] Available at: www.sign.ac.uk/assets/sign114.pdf [Accessed 27 Oct. 2018].

Smyth, L. (2010). *Marian Keyes: 'Depression has turned my life into a living hell'*. [online] The Independent. Available at: www.independent.co.uk/arts-entertainment/books/news/marian-keyes-depression-has-turned-my-life-into-a-living-hell-1858535.html [Accessed 25 Jan. 2019].

Studenthealth.blogs.bristol.ac.uk. (2013). *A student's account of depression | Student health doc blog*. [online] Available at: https://studenthealth.blogs.bristol.ac.uk/2013/06/20/a-students-account-of-depression/ [Accessed 24 Sep. 2018].

Verywell Mind. (2018). *How Many People Are Actually Affected by Depression Every Year?*. [online] Available at: www.verywellmind.com/depression-statistics-everyone-should-know-4159056 [Accessed 17 Sep. 2018].

Weitzman, M., Rosenthal, D. and Liu, Y. (2011). *Paternal Depressive Symptoms and Child Behavioral or Emotional Problems in the United States. PEDIATRICS*, [online] 128(6), pp.1126–34. Available at: www.ncbi.nlm.nih.gov/pubmed/22065273 [Accessed 28 Sep. 2018].

Wootton, D. (2017). *Liam Payne reveals mental health struggle while in 1D*. [online] The Sun. Available at: www.thesun.co.uk/tvandshowbiz/4967618/liam-payne-mental-health-struggle-one-direction/ [Accessed 24 Jan. 2019].

World Health Organization. (2018). *Depression*. [online] Available at: www.who.int/en/news-room/fact-sheets/detail/

depression [Accessed 28 Sep. 2018].

World Health Organization. (2018). *Mental disorders*.
[online] Available at: www.who.int/news-room/fact-sheets/
detail/mental-disorders [Accessed 17 Sep. 2018].

**If you found this book interesting …
why not read these next?**

Doing Single Well

A Guide to Living, Loving and
Dating without compromise

Doing Single Well will help you find fulfilment
in your single life, and if you want a partner,
to wait for one who is right for you.

Body Image Problems
& Body Dysmorphic Disorder

The Definitive Treatment and Recovery Approach

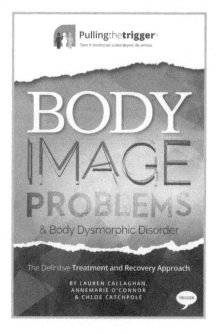

This unique and inspiring book provides simple yet highly
effective self-help methods to help you overcome your body
image concerns and Body Dysmorphic Disorder (BDD).

the *Shaw* **mind**
FOUNDATION

Creating hope for children,
adults and families

Sign up to our charity, The Shaw Mind Foundation

www.shawmindfoundation.org

and keep in touch with us; we would love to hear
from you.

*Our goal is to make help and support available for every
single person in society, from all walks of life.
We will never stop offering hope. These are our promises.*

TRIGGER™

The mental health & wellbeing publisher

www.triggerpublishing.com

Trigger is a publishing house devoted to opening conversations about mental health. We tell the stories of people who have suffered from mental illnesses and recovered, so that others may learn from them.

Adam Shaw is a worldwide mental health advocate and philanthropist. Now in recovery from mental health issues, he is committed to helping others suffering from debilitating mental health issues through the global charity he co-founded, The Shaw Mind Foundation. www.shawmindfoundation.org

Lauren Callaghan (CPsychol, PGDipClinPsych, PgCert, MA (hons), LLB (hons), BA), born and educated in New Zealand, is an innovative industry-leading psychologist based in London, United Kingdom. Lauren has worked with children and young people, and their families, in a number of clinical settings providing evidence based treatments for a range of illnesses, including anxiety and obsessional problems. She was a psychologist at the specialist national treatment centres for severe obsessional problems in the UK and is renowned as an expert in the field of mental health, recognized for diagnosing and successfully treating OCD and anxiety related illnesses in particular. In addition to appearing as a treating clinician in the critically acclaimed and BAFTA award-winning documentary *Bedlam*, Lauren is a frequent guest speaker on mental health conditions in the media and at academic conferences. Lauren also acts as a guest lecturer and honorary researcher at the Institute of Psychiatry Kings College, UCL.

Please visit the link below:
www.triggerpublishing.com

Join us and follow us...

@triggerpub
@Shaw_Mind

Search for us on Facebook